ALTERNATOR

ALTERNATOR

POEMS

CHRIS BANKS

NIGHTWOOD EDITIONS

2023

Nightwood Editions
P.O. Box 1779
Gibsons, BC VON 1V0
Canada
www.nightwoodeditions.com

COVER DESIGN: Angela Yen
TYPOGRAPHY: Libris Simas Ferraz / Onça Design

Nightwood Editions acknowledges the support of the Canada Council for the Arts, the Government of Canada, and the Province of British Columbia through the BC Arts Council.

This book has been printed on 100% post-consumer recycled paper.

Printed and bound in Canada.

LIBRARY AND ARCHIVES CANADA CATALOGUING IN PUBLICATION
Title: Alternator / Chris Banks.
Names: Banks, Chris, 1970- author.
Identifiers: Canadiana (print) 20230444458 | Canadiana (ebook) 20230444474 |
    ISBN 9780889714588 (softcover) | ISBN 9780889714595 (EPUB)
Subjects: LCGFT: Poetry.
Classification: LCC PS8553.A564 A79 2023 | DDC C811/.6—dc23

for Aura

... The self, we shall say, can never be
Seen with a disguise, and never be seen without one.

— MARK STRAND

Writing is like firing a nail gun into the center of a vanity mirror.

— KIM ADDONIZIO

Contents

PART III MIRROR BOUQUET

PART I
CORE SAMPLES OF THE
LATE-CAPITALIST DREAM

Core Samples of the Late-Capitalist Dream

Reality is not paint-by-number. *Show.*
Don't sell. My castle I built out of twigs

when I was four. I still feel under siege
by rising gas prices. Major depression's

relentless trebuchet. I need an alternate.
An understudy. Death is an acquired taste.

I drank sorrow's nectar, until I remembered
happiness is not cheating on taxes, but knowing

joy requires no bucket list. The red curtains
are rising. I am uncertain of my lines.

Even though I play the hero, I improvise
on stage until the ghost within me speaks.

§

Who needs Hell, or a classical underworld
when you have a shuttered Walmart

in your neighbourhood. A corporate
tombstone painted slate grey. *Here lies*

greed and consumption, says the empty
parking lot. Concrete blocks poke up

through grey drifts, marking graves
of unknown cashiers. When you die

may you die, and not rematerialize wearing
a superstore smock. Shopping carts

sit empty in light snow like metal vertebrae
of some creature made extinct long ago.

§

Memory is a tax-free savings account.
On a scale of demon to angel, I am a man.

I am more Lilliputian than Gulliver.
More Popeye than Plato. More K-car

than limousine. Let's rebrand poetry
I Can't Believe It's Not Prose!

Familiar signposts show every road
leads between childhood and the grave.

I tried to be more real, but I ended up
a hunter-gatherer of successive surprises.

Love is hanging towels, side by side,
on the back of a bedroom door.

§

A lady wearing a tattered winter coat
pushes a little stroller of recyclables

down the street, rifling through
bins for wine bottles. A bus driver

pulls over to a glass shelter, argues
with a man to put on a mask.

A billionaire goes on getting richer—
rides a rocket to space. A teenager

trudges through wet snow listening to
an indie playlist. Crust of a white moon,

cutting through darkness, hangs above
the fallen city. A poet's heirloom.

§

Emergency rooms and dive bars are filling up
with February's patrons. Strangers huddle

outside a chain restaurant waiting for a taxi
to shuttle them home to bed. A few homeless

sleep in heated ATM lobbies. People are dying.
People whose last touch is a paramedic's hands.

In a few more sleepless hours, downtown will be
a neon graveyard, or an abandoned movie set.

But for now, the populace is fighting over
who will pay for the cheque, who will go home

with whom. The cold predictably indifferent.
The cold knowing it will eventually win.

§

We try to find our place in feelings
large and small, in algorithms,

online fads, zodiac signs, ancient
patterning of the stars. Who is

speaking here? Launder your
illusions. We are entities of light

more than pronouns. Every person
is a person of interest. Stand in

a police lineup. When the detective
calls your name, step forward,

state your guilty plea. Admit the world is
a faithful mirror, looking through us.

§

All new shops opening downtown
either sell coffee or cannabis.

To indicate something different
requires more than words and ideas

murmuring, like doves, across a page.
Give it to me straight, Doctor!

and she does, writing a prescription
on a tiny white pad for blue pills

that cure sadness, but not restless
imagination syndrome. Side effects

include beliefs, gazing at night skies
knowing you, too, are a fallen star.

§

Over in suburbia, city plows have not made it
down the impassable streets and cul-de-sacs.

Children clamber over snowdrifts on their way
to school. Someone's tongue touches an icicle.

Awe flares momentarily to life. Parts of ourselves,
memories we lost, lie buried in frozen backyards.

The soccer fields across from the man-made pond
look like the afterlife: a blank, unpeopled expanse.

Why do we think there is more? Most of our lives
are spent convincing ourselves we are human,

unlike other animals who do not need Xanax,
birthday candles, art or poems to exist.

§

Trauma is playing a piano
with an iron hammer, a machete.

Each of us carries *A Little Golden Book
of Hurts* deep within us. Yes,

someone you love deeply will suffer
papercuts turning every anguished page.

My encyclopedia entry on suffering
is one word: *Ouch!* If you can't

roll with the constant sucker punches,
brace for impact. To survive life's ordeals,

remember, even the biggest giants,
like Goliath, are felled in time.

§

Maybe I need another tattoo: maybe you do.
A snake wrapped around a sword, or perhaps

a skull. A *memento mori* commemorating
democracy. I keep hoping for a Groupon

for world peace. Alas, no one gets a discount
on pain. I love the marquee of tattoo parlours.

The high-vaulted ceilings of the universe.
The Sistine Chapel. Just don't ask me to paint it!

Real estate prices are core samples of the late-
capitalist dream. A school needs a new name,

one not linked to genocide, but don't worry:
the mascot is still there, cheering you from the sidelines.

§

Some books spend years on shelves
without being touched. Snow blankets

an abandoned driving range.
The motel sign says, *No Vaccination,*

No Vacancy. A horse and buggy
waits in the parking lot of Home Depot.

Across town, citizens are thinking
they need their heads examined.

A psychiatrist researches Bollywood stars
between patients. *I like school!*

says my youngest child, closing his eyes.
He dreams of being a ventriloquist.

§

The meteorologists state it is minus-thirty
which is why the air we breathe in

feels like tiny shards of polar glass.
Thick falling flakes drop white sheaves,

ice on everything. Winter reminds us
reality is not for the weak, for those

without a jacket, or a pair of red mittens,
or a black balaclava to hide exactly who we are.

Hold your unsheathed hand out, and let
snowflakes burn against your palm.

In moments of transformation, in the eye
of eternity's storm, try to live.

§

As snow melts,
orange pylons

punctuate city streets
where fire trucks race

through intersections,
late for some arrival,

sirens blaring, alarming
stray cats hiding

under front porches,
ears flattened

as if they, too, sense smoke—
civilization burning.

§

Spring in the neighbourhood
means couches left curbside,

hopeful gardens. A neighbour
snakes a large rubber hose

into the street, pumps water
from an in-ground pool

to the sewer. I wish I could
flush the bilge of

this era. Two mated ducks
circle pools all afternoon,

watching people rush outside,
shake angry fists at the sky.

§

Taxi drivers have bigger brains than me.
My hippocampus fails to navigate

celebrity birthdays, family dinners,
political outrage, the pursuit of money.

Handprints on a bay window. Clearly, we all want
outside. A jay squawks. A new reformation

is emerging! My brain rewires itself
in spring sunshine. Is the past

a vintage pop-up? A curio-shop of junk?
Or a seashell we sadly outgrew?

Hark, the volta! Choose your weapon:
the cha-cha or the yo-yo?

§

A cherry blossom is its own epiphany.
All my friends from the '90s

grew up to be novelists, poets, suicides.
I do not understand physics, how

planes stay airborne, or the science of
alarm clocks, electric cars, Tylenol gel caps.

But I do understand that every green thought
is an attempt to grapple what is essentially

uncontainable: the panoramic striptease
of human frailty. Friend or foe?

I want for nothing, and still I add
memory and desire to my cart.

§

Angst is jetlag without a passport.
Civil discourse is having an estate sale.

Religion v. Science is making a comeback
on television news. I politely decline

free samples of fascism. Gay conversion therapy.
Headless mannequins huddle in storerooms

after the department stores close down.
Tomorrow's daily special is more

climate change with a side of spite.
A town fountain is full of nickels and dimes.

Make a wish. Toss a coin. Watch it sink.
Hope's secret password is hope.

§

How did you get this number?
Please, stop selling me

gun violence, neoliberalism, nuclear families
in packs of four. *Knock-knock.*

The world's on fire. This isn't a joke.
Think of poetry as a burn unit.

Let's start over. Let's engineer joy!
Create a new architecture for happiness.

In time, friendships wither away.
My nametag says *Writ in Water.*

Close your eyes and write the next line.
Start your own *Odyssey* home.

§

Small is beautiful.
Would you like to supersize that sentiment?

First thought, plain thought.
You have my permission to disrupt language.

Was is a chorus that never arrives.
Even humming it, we get it wrong.

Most poems are in the key of sleep.
Truth emanates from lived experience.

I wind up my brain's cuckoo clock
in the hopes some bird will sing.

Evening rain evaporates like old cartoons.
Like child pop stars. Like *Civil Elegies*.

§

Unfettered rain slips from grey skies.
Anxiety is a private firing squad of fears.

America keeps breaking up with progress.
Depression costs fifty bucks a month.

The middle class is fast becoming
an urban legend. Inflation is on the run.

July festivals. Vegetable patches.
Dogs and toddlers dying in hot cars.

The rain finally stops. An antidote
to permanence. To gloom's cheap façade.

A UPS van cruises up and down the street
delivering boxes. The word *enough* is out of stock.

§

Someone sips a summer daiquiri.
The photographer is here!

Everyone crowds in for the picture.
Say apple pie! Say bougainvillea!

Death clicks his camera. A relative dies.
This is how time functions.

COVID is a terrible game of tag.
More money or more health?

Fold a napkin into origami.
Mistake it for true gold.

I'm not ready to give up on beauty.
I'll take even these few crumbs.

§

No struggle, no epiphany.
A girl draws a sun in yellow chalk.

Rats live under my garden shed.
The invisible world is here!

I need a private tutor to teach me
the real meaning of happiness.

The neighbourhood is alive.
Dogs barking, kids laughing.

The girl draws a hopscotch
game on the sidewalk.

Carefully, she hops on one foot,
trying to avoid the future.

Falling leaves in October.
So many desiccated colours!

All things bonding us
to this mortal life break.

I yank books from shelves
looking for a line, or a quick wit

to tell me how best to live.
The wind blows, and more

leaves make the leap! You think
I'm grasping for answers

when really all I want is to lean
into language, and let go.

PART II
SAY DYNAMITE

Versailles

There is a Versailles of the human heart. A palace castled
in our innermost thoughts. The world enlarges, diminishes,
based on how many bodies our bodies have touched. Make
feelings a crusade. Surveil your desires. Find one's riches
amidst all the blood and sunshine and anguished liaisons.
Do not abbreviate love's vocabulary. When the guillotines
are finally erected, when the rabble storms the palisades,
torches and sabres in hand, shouting chaos, rioters waving
pamphlets like flags in the streets, whisper love in all its
many colours. Open its fortress doors. Plunder its rooms
to find amongst the large oil paintings and boudoir chairs,
the heart's wants. That bounty waiting to be carried away.

Love Song

I'm all for sturdy beginnings like the opening chords
of "Crimson and Clover," the Tommy James original
or the Joan Jett version with its teasing distortion,
the latter bringing me back to grade eight dances.
If you're waiting for a chorus, I am sorry to tell you
this is not a song. Not even close. *Yeah... I'm not
such a sweet thing...* is an invisible button I have
pinned to my chest wherever I go. It's Friday all day
and phone scammers have only phoned me twice
demanding money for tax evasion. *Show me yours,
and I'll show you mine* is my short take on the senses
and the imagination. Pinky swear. Love, sickness,
English gardens, tie-dyed T-shirts... I'm all in. Totes.
Can you keep a secret? Alright this is a song of sorts.
The verse we have reached is full of astral systems
and flight plans. The melody changes the pH levels
in the oceans, and the universe happily claps along.
My day job includes eating bananas, and unspecified
aches in my joints. Getting older is a slow rotisserie
of bills and panic attacks you are forced to eat. At
least the beauty of this world survives as we age,
no matter how much we try to dismantle its allure
with new condo builds and payday loan stores.
Thank you for the boutonnière. After the dance,
we begin to go our separate ways but I take you

home with me, your breath on my neck a silent
memento I never told anyone about until now.

Say Dynamite

Say Moon. Say Dynamite. Say Imago. The last stage an insect
goes through in metamorphosis. Say the Pixies' *Doolittle.*
Say "This Monkey's Gone to Heaven." Say what you mean.
Call 1-800-WAKE-UP. Operators standing by. Do you
feel trapped inside this mineshaft? What we call the soul
stays hidden, but its walk-in music is part angelic choir, part
"Hells Bells." My fight card is full. My record is five love affairs.
Two mental breakdowns. *I'm a good person, I'm a good person,*
drones the record player inside of me. If this were true, I'd
be doing more to end hunger. Or word hunger. Say *Cat's
Cradle.* Say starlight. Apotheosis. Past and future are different
frequencies playing classic oldies, and tomorrow's pet deaths.
Call me a religious syncretist, but let's place the Romantics
and the Surrealists in a blender. Apollinaire, Wordsworth.
Dean Young and Shelley. I wandered lonely as a nail gun in
search of a cloud. Look on my mighty koi pond and despair!
You see, I'm scared to say anything too plainly. Language
is a crash cart, reviving lifeless things. Say dollhouse. Say profit
margins. Say Jupiter's rings. I speak fluent fight or flight.
I may be lost, but I love the meander. The path more than
the destination. The word truth more than its hollow echo.
If you put your faith in me, I promise to deliver a morning sky
strung out on Valium. A stockpile of flowers. Carnations,
not cancer. Azaleas, not arsenic. This is my idea nursery,
so please quietly rock each one gently against your chest.

Let's make a pact. You be you, and I'll be me: the planet can ignore us both. Say sweetheart. Sweetheart.

The Garden of Human Delights

Not that I ogle Rubens' nudes any more
than the next guy, but nudity in oil paintings
really shows us what we gave up when
we closed the gate on Eden and put on
clothes. Everyone has a recurring dream
about being naked and embarrassed at work.
The Pope is no different. The only exceptions
are blissed-out nudists playing volleyball
who would not recognize a crucifixion
from a church lady driving nine-inch nails
through their limbs with disapproving eyes.
In the '70s, people got naked in musicals
and it changed nothing. I look at some
priests and wonder if they will implode
from human longing. Sex should be viewed
less as a dirty little business of feathered boas
and flavoured oils and more a communiqué,
a telegram sent between distant galaxies.
The message: I know you. I trust you.
Let's be more to each other than a drive-by
transaction of spermatozoa. At least tonight.
We can decide in the morning if a lifetime
of snuggling, arguing over who washed
the dishes last, is for us. My girlfriend
tells me I need to write more poems

about sex, but the Angel of Suffering
keeps telling me I'll go blind from all
the innuendo and erections. Maybe
there is a garden of human delights
for sale down the street. Maybe we can
match the asking price if we combine
our incomes. Maybe we can live there.
Maybe be happy. Despite the thorns.

Ode to a Broken World

I can't even with the white noise of yada yada yada.
The hunger for more more more. Consciousness has
wandered the desert of my body for over fifty years.
You can quote Descartes or Shakespeare or Kafka
and still some mornings your mouth fills with the ash
of an overpromised, undervalued life. Art the ax
unable to break the frozen sea within. I sought peace
of mind. Not a mind in pieces. Not white orgies of
political discord. Not toxic allegiances to a country
or to Holy Scriptures. Not this sad eulogizing of
yesterday. Not nostalgia's leitmotif. Not a World
Wide Web full of prophetic delusions. Not ruined
ghettos in our cities, but teenagers with ghetto blasters
on every block. Not you, not me, but us together
withstanding the crescendos of our shared delusions.
Not this hoarding of wealth among those who breed
billions in the Cayman Islands. Not lies and promises,
but the unwavering authenticity of seeing the world
with one's own eyes. No one else's. That prismatic
understanding. That inner drug. That symphonic
upwelling of *Yes!* We crave those moments while
rowing across the Lethe of another workweek,
another month, another year. Our sitting atop
mountains of plunder and thinking ourselves poor.

Reality

It was easier as a kid with a bug-hunting net
and a little jar with holes in the lid capturing
iridescent grasshoppers and yellow bumblebees.
I'm thinking reality has something to do with
rhizomes or sequined tube tops or staying
inside your body for nearly a hundred years
if you are lucky. The photographs do not
really do it justice. All those family portraits
of sunsets and sullen grandparents. What
about bioluminescent creatures constellating
like stars deep within the Mariana Trench?
What about the bird dive-bombing everyone
who gets too close to its nest? Easy to pull
things apart but so much harder to stitch
it all back together to see the big picture.
Let us break the fourth wall that exists
between ourselves and the ocean. Between
the interior of the car with its little heater
spitting out warmth and the blizzard outside.
I am not one for religion but I do know
you cannot 3D-print the soul. Scientists
say there are at least thirty-six alien civilizations
in the Milky Way alone, which is fucked.
Choices: ice cream or the God particle?
I go for a jog managing to skirt the grass

and flowerbeds. I stay on the sidewalk yet
somehow contain multitudes of dreams.
Cast your net wide knowing whatever
that buzzing is, deep in the honeysuckle
and clover, it might just sting you.

I Don't Like Philosophy

If you turned me insight out, you would
find my id strangling my superego, or is it
the other way around? Psychology really
should be the study of sighs. Like when
a person stares at a cloud, or a medical
centre in a business park, then exhales:
what are they thinking? I prefer vistas
over Visa cards. Buy low. Sell high. Get rich.
Scientists need to huddle up and figure out
a way to end capitalism, its slow murder party.
Wearing a copper bracelet does not prevent
arthritis, or white men with guns from killing
unarmed Black men on television news.
Society needs a showrunner. We won't find
answers in books. Better to look inside
our hearts, there beneath the pit bull snarls
and rock 'n' roll and microaggressions.
Stop selling me things! I want to be free
to read poems, to raise a few children,
to sway in a light warm breeze where facts
and hard truths won't stand in the way
of my breathing in and out, which works
better for me than other plans to learn
a second language or keep tigers as pets.
This is all I am saying even if most of it

gets lost in the talk of sparrows and rivers
and death that just confuses the subject.
I'm not one for philosophy but unfortunately
it likes me—not as a theory—but as a person
who eats Mini-Wheats and worries about
the shucking of his mortal coil, or why am I
not a tree. Huddled alone inside Plato's cave,
my imagination keeps me company.

Interrogation Room A

Tell us your whereabouts when the blue macaw went
extinct? The white rhino? Is capitalism working, yes or no?
Is heaven a podcast of lies? Does sky-gazing make you
an accessory to existence? Name your accomplice, fear
or laughter? Explain the Big Bang to us one more time.
Give it to us straight. Is a nest of bees a papier-mâché
cathedral? Is a hurricane an engine of rage? Do words
like *crocus*, *spiderweb*, *chlorophyl* mean anything to you?
Why are you fidgeting? We can place you at the scene
of your birth. What body lies atop this pyre of drafts?
If the murder weapon was a flaming sword, does that
make you an angel or a serial killer? We have proof
God is a photo on a bulletin board's most wanted list.
Why did you burn the dictionaries? We need you
to cooperate if we are going to take down yesterday
and tomorrow. The moment is in witness protection.
Let me ask you, how well do you know your shadow?
Would you be willing to wear a wire? We need to get
the full moon on tape. You are looking at a lifetime
of washing dishes and second-guessing your career.
The facts are building a case for scars, more nudity
and angry swans. Look, we recovered the ransom

of grey clouds and parking lots! The mugshots in
your dreams are damning. The easy way is rain on
a spring morning. The hard way is a fist hammering
piano keys. Listen to the crickets and take the deal.

New Apostles

I tried being an apostle but all the prophets were in jail.
The X-ray glasses did not work. I was born Christian
but now I am some new breed of Romantic. All my visions
are luminous self-portraits. Never mind the talk of clouds,
flowers, Grecian urns. The solicitor says I am in breach
for not using enough rhymes in my work. I feel bad for people
who try to handcuff themselves to a Bible. *Owed* or *odes*,
it is all the same to me. I work then wait for my paycheque
to clear. God is a coyote. Sometimes, I am the cold embers.
Other times, the fire. My imagination moults, then shows off
its new wings. Too bad the world is a fly swatter. Am I a frog
singing at Carnegie Hall, or one being slowly boiled alive?
It changes week to week. A poem is an oath of eloquence.
A deep dive into syllables, images and bad TV reception.
Why can't I just change the channel? Wrong answers only.
Even a nutshell is palatial if you can adjust your mindset.
Aging is a state of being deprogrammed from the past.
How did I get this job, closed-captioning the unseeable?
I love where this is heading, whether it be another award,
or a few handfuls of dirt being thrown onto a wooden
box. I'm looking for someone to teach me to be joyous
without intercepting my free will. Without me having
to go witness door to door. Nothing lasts says the major
chord strummed on the guitar. Strum it again. Can I get
a Hallelujah? An Amen? *No, dummy,* says the darkness.

My index of paradoxes is longer than my list of prayers.
I have taken a lifetime vow of public speaking. Too bad
my audience has no ears. If you are ever in a boat during
a storm, and a figure begins to walk upon the waves
towards you, I suggest you row, or end up martyred,
or worse, a teacher. *Heresy* or *hearsay*, I speak the truth.

Ode to Disappearing

Here be dragons. The god in the machine
has escaped and is roaming the theatre.
Tiny gizmos created in Chinese factories
help to alleviate boredom. Suicide by ennui
is not really a thing. Scientists have detected
patterns in radio signals from deep space.
The scissors are missing. MYSTERIES
in all caps gets you no closer to the truth.
Kids playing in a sprinkler are one example
of *Spiritus Mundi*. The bulbs you planted
last summer coming into bloom, another.
I find you enchanting and would love to
sleep nose to nose with you. Things fall
apart, beautifully. A plant that last flowered
when woolly mammoths walked the Earth,
found buried in permafrost, gets a second
chance to die. Is not life grand? My inner
rough beast slouches towards bedtime.
Yeats was a genius, but a profoundly sad
person with no access to happy little pills.
My prescription needs refilling. Blue skies
and Abilify keep me upright. The jukebox
is broken, so I hum a little Lucinda Williams
while getting the milk. "Sailing to Byzantium"
is a fight song for MFA programs. No one

calls collect any more. What is the boiling
point for possibilities? For lost potential?
I would rather gamble money on this world,
no matter how ruined. The teller behind
shatterproof glass hands back your change,
then forgets you. Take it as a blessing.

Penny Arcade

The penny arcades are no longer accepting pennies.
Climate change is like slow dancing on the *Titanic*
after its screaming argument with an iceberg. Once
the water reaches your trousers, it is already too late.
I burned down the art school. Certainty scares away
what surprise feeds on, like a wolf wearing a cowbell
stalking mule deer. Building a poem is like building
a spiderweb without spinnerets, so instead of silk,
you are stuck with popsicle sticks, coloured yarn
and too much glue. The resemblances are striking.
I need a dialysis machine for my too-human anxiety.
A little blood circulation, butterflies and pizazz
go a long away in making me feel like a real artist.
A poet who brought a flashlight to a pillow fight.
Like a thirteenth-century astronomer discovering
the absence of celestial spheres. Plato, you idiot!
Wisdom second-hand is still wisdom. There is no
rewind button to life, so breathe and pace yourself.
Try singing some '80s pop, or playing gin rummy
with the imagination. Pay the ransomware but know
it will not necessarily restore your immortal soul,
or the glory days of English departments. Usually
when someone takes a scythe to the purple irises,
I am the first one to pick up the fallen blooms.

Have you read this anthology of smoke? Fire's
New and Selected Flames? When you are done,
put out the embers, but don't leave me alone.
My coupons for mere living are forfeit in the dark.

The Halftime Show Is on Fire

I am dedicated to watering vegetables and my own
angst. I leave naming the outer planets and the sex
lives of Romans for another day. A man who built
his own rocket, and believed the earth is flat, crashed
into the desert and died. I wonder if he saw the curvature
of the planet before all systems failed. Why are there
so many conspiracy theorists multiplying daily online,
preaching Revelations, aborted babies, faux vaccines?
Everyone has to believe in something, but why not love
which is not password protected. An era of eros. Not
pandemics. It is simple and still we get it wrong. On TV
this morning, America is burning. America is burning,
and white supremacists are wearing funny red hats
that say *Make Whites Great Again.* Nothing is funny
when a Black man is dead, and cities are on fire.
I wear my whiteness like a Hawaiian shirt which is
to say on the periphery of others' suffering so now
I am both sad and privileged, a feeling I cannot shake
no matter what I say about wisteria or Catullus or
halftime shows. The halftime show is on fire
so why are we still in our seats, some of us even

applauding? Do we even know what we are doing? When I watch the video of the cop pressing his knee against a Black man's throat, I find it hard to breathe. Hard to breathe, but I'm the one breathing, believing the lie. The white lie there is nothing to be done.

Chariots of Fire

All that synth and piano and pining hope.
I want to build a better mousetrap, but
Hamlet lies dead, poisoned on the floor
of Elsinore, the royal family of Denmark
wiped out, so cancel my ambassadorship.
What does $x + y$ amount to? Coleridge
wrote "Kubla Khan" then stopped writing
at thirty. Taking long walks, drinking
laudanum by the pint, is no substitute
for tying oneself to a desk, or following
the snakes and ladders of inspiration.
The sign on the road says the sublime
is organic. Raspberries pick your own.
You need to do the work even if your
fingers come away stained red. Even
if you get desire's tiny seeds stuck
between your teeth. I thought I was
a Romantic for the longest time, until
I got kicked out of the hiking club,
then crushed a flower under my boot,
which is sad since Realism is no longer
taking members, unless you agree to
spritz everything with hand sanitizer,
and then dry-hump verisimilitude.
I wouldn't want to belong to a club

that would have me as a member,
said Groucho Marx who is now
a member of the growing consortium
of the dead. I try to belong to places,
but wobble around ice rinks. I drink
water in bars. I call God a ghost
to his absent face. At least no one
has poured poison in the porches
of my ears. F-stop or full stop?
One is filled with music. The other
a stony silence that wants us to don
our overcoats, empty the building.

Alternator

Most things are made of wood, plastic, aluminum,
copper, glass. I would rather things were made of
ocean spray, grass scent, sunlight, human longing.
Science says we are all malformed celestial debris,
but no one ever resuscitates a meteorite, do they?
Give me the CliffNotes. This map of the universe
has no index of affinities. My syllabus is full up of
French symbolist poets, UFO sightings. I show
my devotion to this world by collecting everything,
which is a fool's hobby. Spinoza said, *All things
excellent are as difficult as they are rare.* I need a tuning
fork for the real. A rain check for the miraculous.
I tried each thing too, Mr. Ashbery, but only some
things come à la carte. The mind is an alternator.
What I know and what I don't know weigh
the same as *nuisance* and *numinous.* To speak truly,
there is no design unless grown from a petri dish.
Less certainties, more collages! So many varieties
of life, but only one death! Millions of years of
evolution, and what do I do with it? I attempt
to thread fire through the eye of my imagination.
Silly, I know. The way the seasons keep changing
the subject, and I'm always getting burned. But
sometimes a dress of flame hangs in the dark,
sometimes I even see someone wearing it!

Territorial

A bird that went extinct recently evolved itself
back into existence. Take that, natural selection!
I am evolving by trimming my beard once a week,
and no longer cringing when I see orcas hunting
seals on television. Circle of life is a polite term
for Nature's never-ending bloodsport. Time is
the real predator. Its diet of nostalgia and tears.
The bags under my eyes tell me I'm not a kid,
a fourteen-year-old dancing to Prince songs in
a high school gymnasium anymore. My incisors
tell me I'm an apex carnivore. My father and I used
to hunt grouse, but all the guns and shooting felt
like terrible things to put on a résumé. I would
rather highlight coral reefs, angels drifting between
Heaven and Hell, Keats' letters, Darla who first
kissed me. The stars revolving around our heads.
If I hunt anything, it's the fine edges of one thing
fitting into another thing. That click! My fingers
running along invisible seams. My habitat includes
sparkling water, shrimp ceviche, long steamy baths.
Flat-screen TVs and writing elegies for childhood
are just the way I mark my territory. The birds
in the backyard change their tunes when a cat
wanders out from behind a shed. There's danger
in forgetting life is mortal and organic, meaning

millions of skin cells are regenerating, my body
replacing itself every seven years with another,
a facsimile equipped with dreams and memories
and now that I think about it, no ripcord.
Just this falling, flailing towards certain death,
and me trying to become air the whole way down.

Moving Target

You can't hit a moving target, said the young man
inside the old man's body. I looked at him, imagining
all the parties, all the celebrations, all the huzzahs,
all the investments, all the deaths, all the births,
all the high school examinations, all the ice cream socials,
all the candlelit dinners, all the beaches, all the sunsets,
all the magazines piled high beside a La-Z-Boy recliner,
all the dogs petted and buried, all the church masses,
all the Boxing Day sales, the scotches before bed,
all the good deeds, all the extravagant guilt,
all the days, all the nights, all the in-between,
all the shooing of squirrels from bird feeders,
all the hours standing in front of a mirror shaving,
all the bewildering labour spent in pursuit of money,
all the parades, weddings, funerals and expenses,
all the untranslatable seconds, all the signatures,
all the promising career paths that went bust,

all the first kisses, all the hugging, all the cruelty,
all the joys, like crickets kept in a bamboo cage,
all the world crumbling a little more each day,
all the warning labels, all the looming projects,
all the hard deadlines, all the tree-lined avenues,
all the smoke, the campfires, the spelunking sins,
all the desires, problems served up on a half shell,
all the right words for the wrong occasions,
all the wrestling torment of knotting syllables,
all the murky moments stitched into a golden tapestry,
all the testimonials, all the dog and pony shows,
all the lost members of his tribe—all gone, adios—
and him still moving, slowly, but with great care
through the garden among the dragonflies,
the gun barrel of time tracking him relentlessly,
and he not quite caught within its sight.

Karaoke Machine

Follow the bouncing ball of late-stage capitalism.
Too bad you can't sing along to it.
This poem is sans Wi-Fi so stop asking
for my password. What emotion
did I leave unleashed in the backyard
all afternoon? Just ask the kids next door.
They want their baseball back, and blue oceans.
This is a field guide for old commercial jingles.
My French maid costume is worn at the seams.
This party is going to last another three decades.
Sadly, friends, the karaoke machine is broken.
Dictionaries and encyclopedias, once indispensable,
now lie spine-ripped, beached on shelves
in classrooms. Somewhere, a Bay Street lawyer
is screaming into a phone, *Do you know who I am?*
Somewhere, a child is huddled inside a closet.
I'm the reluctant author of this latest round
of scandalous exposés. The war approaches.
The virus spans continents, utility bills arrive.
We are a slow IV drip of chance encounters.
I may not know what the basement switch is for,
but of this, I am sure: ignore your notifications.
Order blood tests. Some day you may be forced
to offer up your body. To bleed for a diagnosis.
I would breathe fire, but it requires eating fire.

Ready or not, here I come, armed with a mic.
A hit playlist that might make you scream.

Sublimity

The sublime is hidden behind a paywall. Play its glory
backwards, and all you hear is clichés. The sublime is
a Dutch landscape painting of peasants toiling in a field
trying to harvest a few gold coins. The sublime is a lock of
God's hair kept in a brooch hidden beneath the Pope's robes.
The sublime is the sound made when inner and outer worlds
collide. The sublime is a selfless exorcism. The sublime is
semi-divine, but knows nothing about demigods or crosses.
The sublime is the first book to pick the lock of your memory
using nothing more than its words. The sublime is a balm
to sooth everyday ills: misfortune, debt, anxiety and grief.
The sublime is embarrassing, but beautiful. The sublime will
not bloom if left unwatered. Mix in human experience
and fetterless ambition. The sublime is no manufactory.
The sublime is no farm of heart or mind. It is the first breath
of fresh air one breathes after some play, or novel, or sunset
tears the vacuum seal of your spirit wide open. The sublime
prefers the word *orchid* over *ennui*. The king's coffers empty.
The poet's thoughts full. If you try to bear-hug the sublime,
you will be left holding nothing but your dread. Doff fears.
The sublime happens when the typist stops listening to others.
Track it in your peripheral vision. Bait it with thoughts of
immortality. With pomp and ceremony. Roll out the red
carpet. Holler *Genius!* in the empty palace. The sublime
sings the delirium of its golden ode. Even when nothing is left,

when opium and fever dreams have taken your best years,
and you walk into the bright morning, stifled with sunshine,
the words all gone, and you cannot bear to describe the loss
in all its painful exactitude anymore, the sublime yells, *More!*

Resemblances

After Bob Hicok

I've decided I look like a ham radio, or if not a ham radio,
someone controlling a dial, speaking into a microphone
late at night, breathing, *Who's out there, over?* I also look
like a crumbling medieval castle whose moat has been
drained, a fancy pen that smudges, a petty dictator. Even
an army of hummingbirds. To be merely a human being
is to be a thimble of troubles. A music box of impulses.
The one always hungry to be two. I aspire to be better at
multiplying images: to be a meadow, or at least a person
who would lay down in one amongst clover, honeysuckle
and dragonflies. To be a glass skyscraper. A mirrored hive
of productivity. To be the match. And the lit candle. To be
the river, and the current pushing it forward. When I was
a kid, I only wanted to be freckle-free, better at sports;
to pass my grades, maybe kiss a girl or two. Now, I want
to be the whole earth, spinning and spinning, in a centrifuge
of language. To free words from their objects. No ideas
but in essences. Candy and cave paintings. The garden
and the serpent within it. Once I wished to be a mountain,
but instead I grew up to be a gnome. A fountain of want.
A robot on call. Sometimes, when it is particularly quiet,
I even feel like an empty bandshell, desperate for music.
Or a street market full of nothingness. Or an angel who
hates religious talk. Just follow my voice down the well,
and you too can be an old hat full of sorrows, a watch

abandoned in a drawer, a greeting card faded, an ancient
message of love. Tell me who I approximate now.

PART III
MIRROR BOUQUET

I NEVER READ Berryman's *77 Dream Songs* or Lowell's *Notebook*
but here I am, improvising a long sequence, trying not to leave
anything out, my intelligence a little restless, my imagination
all-inclusive. I am hoping to put the *then* back in authentic,
the *now* back in knowledge, my concerns free-ranging and
arbitrary, although I am the first to admit I am not ideally
suited to restraint, when it is amplitude, expansiveness I seek,
outfitting my poems with pennies on train tracks, absinthe in
Prague, black flies in June, death on repeat. I want to pack it all in;
everything I mean. The highs and lows. The kitchen sink. I cannot
tell if I am fussy, or not fussy, already eleven lines deep, and still
I have said nothing about Mars, Japanese ghosts or prizes
in cereal boxes. So I sacrifice a little intensity for immensity,
trying to piece together a Tower of Babel that won't fall down.

WOULD YOU JUST LOOK at the time? I am fifty, and the Amazon is burning. I am fine with getting older, but truth be told, I do miss the clueless wonder of childhood innocence. Me, at two, mistaking my shadow for a hulking gorilla keeping me trapped in my bedroom. Me, at thirteen, playing ninjas in the forest while my grandfather succumbed to cancer. Adolescence was not the liberation I thought it would be. All the experts say I am well-adjusted, and turned out okay, even if my face fits more loosely than it once did. I guess what I miss most about being a child is their conception of time. How summers could last five years. Grade three was a decade and a half. Time speeds up as you get older, so pull out the stops, aerate the wine, have the sex, do the drugs, bury your beloveds. *My advice*, says time, *is to hurry the hell up*.

FUCK THE TAO. Give me carrot cake and key lime pie instead. The way to order one's own life is by ordering more dessert. I believed in it when I was younger. Felt there was an ultimate reality I could glean through pain and sweat and experience. Now I just want cheese-filled crust for my pizza. I have not exactly given up. Just given in to shopping at big-box stores. To next-day deliveries of cat litter and late-night impulses. I know this sounds terrible. I know I should be more enlightened, be a keen connoisseur of yoga and *élan*, of warmed-over spiritual platitudes, but the way of the universe is not a path. It is more an inventory, a catalogue of blunders and begonias, of Pachelbel and air conditioning, of protests and politics, and the sum of my wisdom is this: eat more dessert.

DO YOU MIND if I get personal? The *I* is just a placeholder
in this poem anyway. The self that writes *Truth is simply*
a kingdom of telling, not of facts is not the self that will
read this a day later, crossing out words, adding new ones,
hoping it all leads to some sort of elegance or understanding,
which sounds boring and ordinary, I know—the *I* knows
what it knows—but at least the words come out half-right
in the declining light, though few care as passionately as me,
the me who wants to be moved by poems, me who wants to know
all the ways of knowing what people think about outer planets
and clouds and windfallen apples. So I read books. The *I* inside
writes some too. Language is the real school. I sit in the back
of the class looking out a window at a small grove of trees
where sits a giant bronze sundial, the hours growing late.

WHAT SHALL WE SAY about this sonnet leaking blood all over the page, whispering old songs and feral emotions? My depression is wrapped in gold leaf, and there is a red coal stuck in my mouth that I wish to spit out. How ignorant I was to think life, poetry, any of it, would be easy. I stand with one foot in the past, the other planted in this late hour, finally knowing what is meant by the cries of the birds circling above a world of strangers. What have I accomplished? I have taught three thousand students to read *Twelfth Night*. My books sit in bookstores waiting for someone to pull them loose, to muddle through their pages. What shall I do in the meantime? Count blessings like so many buttons in a jar? Write new poems some will read, most will forget like yesterday's skinny black leather ties? Think of this as my fluctuating self-portrait. No fire escape once you start down art's hidden corridors, but the end door leads to a rooftop garden. Do not live for nothing. Burn or be burned.

THE SUMMER I TRIED LSD, I lived with two Kims and Bill who took over the basement, four of us sharing a small house. Where we got tabs of acid I don't remember. I just remember sticking it under my tongue, listening to 808 State and Spacemen 3 whose motto was take drugs to make music to take drugs to, watching the dull paisley-patterned wallpaper change to paper dolls dancing, bright colours swirling, strobing on the water-stained ceiling; the one Kim squeezing a small ball, lightly panicking in a corner; the other Kim laughing, offering us all freezies. The mind, it opened like a sunflower under the spell of psychedelics. Boundaries between self and world, subject and object, dissolved, fell away that summer. I remember the Kims and me quietly tripping out, the Hubble Telescope sending its first images back, A.S. Byatt's *Possession* half-read for a literature class with a favourite professor, *Terminator 2* a blockbuster juggernaut smashing box office records. J. Spaceman's voice crooning, *Step into the breeze...*

HOW CAN YOU STAND to tell the truth of yourself? It is mainly smoke and mirrors. A few half-truths misremembered. Really, it is just the essence I am giving you, in a Proustian sense. The past is dead, or at least not here, and what do I really know about truth anyway? What I see is perspective, not the truth, but I think it to be true which is why I talk so much about that boy-child on Monck Hill fist-fighting another boy, or that green kid in university whispering *I love you* in the dorm room's darkness, or now this man thinking about fake news. Marcus Aurelius once said, *Everything we hear is an opinion, not a fact.* Truth is, I know I get truth wrong, but integrity is telling the truth, even the smallest grains, to oneself. Stop hiding evidence. What I am saying is the bodies are in the basement, some are buried in the backyard, and truth is a map I hold inside my flesh and blood. Are you listening? Honesty never felt so good.

DEPRESSION MY OLD FRIEND, bosom buddy, neurocognitive
compatriot, how long has it been? Thirty years! A girl
in university broke up with me, and then you darkened
my door, threw your black cowl around me, so much so
I lost fifteen pounds, had to take Gravol to sleep, then
you were gone for a few years—Montreal, grad school,
South Korea—until surprise! You were back again. I
bought a small Monopoly house on a busy street, and
you moved in. A shitty housemate. We stayed up late
drinking too much beer. I suffered your jeers, your slights,
until you went on walkabout again. Last time you arrived,
you arrived for good. You ended my marriage; clear-cut
my happiness. I finally went to the hospital, and told
doctors you were stalking me. At least meds are free.

THE FIRST GIRL I slept with I wanted to marry. It's the old story
retold, sex equals love, but more pathetic. The next woman
I slept with was because the first girl who broke up with me
did not want me sleeping with the second girl. I had sex with
her anyway, and two others. All were friends. Then there
was a girl from New Mexico, and another girl whom I dated
while having sex with my roommate Nancy. I hurt them all
because I was hurt, or so I told myself, when really I guess
I harboured a suspicion of intimacy, true intimacy, preferring
to drink at a bar, then go home with a stranger or a friend.
I remember sleeping with a woman once, and then a year later,
she asked me to walk onto a sidewalk to watch her smoke,
only to see her tear up because of our silence. I wish I had
comforted her, but ineptitude, not ego, bade me not speak.

NOT THAT I WAS a Lothario, or a Casanova of sorts. Just a weirdo with middling insecurities, disastrous at dating, with modest swag trying to move the plot of my life forward with few attachments. It was only later I trusted myself and others enough to say, *Let's live together and see where it goes...* First, Cass who threw pots and pans onto the floor, and then stormed out of my house, only to become a best friend twenty years later. Next, Teresa to whom I said *I do* and now share my two children with, but no longer a marriage. Finally, Aura unfazed by my drinking history and time in rehab; Aura with her one hundred dresses, and peculiar way of leaving bills in a mailbox weeks at a time. Aura who will never willingly break down a cardboard box, but who peers at me with such love, such gratitude, I feel a fire in my groin, a growing sense of ardour in my heart. The old heart whinnying like a colt.

I WORRY ABOUT my carbon footprint. All those sparkling water cans in the recycling. Better those than beer bottles, I quietly tell myself remembering nights of drinking fourteen Coors and then working the next day, only to do it over again the next night, my memory like a goldfish, my hangovers like so many cloudbursts of pain, until I quit. The blackouts I thought would kill me. And the time students found me drunk on a sidewalk downtown, then drove me home, so I had to shamefacedly talk to them, thank them after class on Monday. What the hell was wrong with me? Addiction, my friends, makes for a terrible dance party. After I quit, it took three years to feel semi-normal, not to wince when someone left a wine glass half-empty or a beer unchaperoned on a table. But truthfully, sobriety is worth it. It punches a few breath-holes in the lid of your soul. Hope a blue Morpho, fluttering within.

THIS IS NOT AN URN of images, nor is it a proper self-depiction. I couch-surfed for years between the ordinary and ecstatic, between my head's penthouse, my heart's studio apartment, waiting for the lived truth to unveil itself. Now I have this double chin, wrinkles like parentheses around my blue eyes, while the everyday and the otherworldly are duking it out in an alley outside. The duende long stopped caring who wins. But I do, or at least I think I do. I'm halfway to the grave, and yet still a boy obsessed with *Jaws* and great white sharks in 1975. A starry-eyed hipster cutting across McGill to get to a poetry workshop at Concordia in the '90s. An alcoholic shivering, sweating in bed… does it even matter when? Caring what other people think is one of my deep interior fears. Take this as insurance and send it to the papers if ever I disappear.

THOSE WERE THE YEARS I slept weekends on Paul's couch in the Annex:
smoked a half-pack of cigarettes Friday and Saturday nights, woke up
smelling of smoke, alcohol, hungover, ringed by books, both hardcover
and homemade, so many collections I would grab a handful of titles
then read in the basement's half-dark beside the low table with DVDs,
a half-eaten pizza. Those years were an apprenticeship. I learned more
on that couch than during my whole MFA. Later, Paul would move
to the Junction, and I helped move all those books across town. Paul
would find love, then lose it, find it again. Just like me. Sometime
along the way, the cigarettes would get tossed. The couch would go
missing. Our friendship would change. I don't know why we go over
old memories like Polaroids in our minds. The sad endings and new
beginnings of the past. I miss that couch. I miss my friend. Paul and I
setting out at night, loudly singing songs, caught in each other's orbit.

MY FIRST POETRY love affair was Al Purdy, then Gwendolyn MacEwen. Writers taught in my Intro to Canadian Poetry class, Gwen already dead two years from trying to quit alcohol without medically detoxing, so I had to borrow her recorded voice from the library's reserve desk, to hear her read poems like "The Red Bird You Wait For," "Manzini: Escape Artist," "Dark Pines Under Water": her work already newly minted Canadian classics. I read her oeuvre by taking an independent reading course. Even read the novels *Julian the Magician* and *King of Egypt, King of Dreams*. I would listen to her voice on vinyl, then stare into her kohl-blackened eyes, thinking about those poems in her last book, *Afterworlds*, ones about the *Tao of Physics*. Purdy was still alive, giving readings. A friend interviewed him; Purdy rowed him about a lake, coaxed him to drink beer because the doctors told Purdy he couldn't. Now they're all dead, their voices just this spooky action at a distance.

I WILL SAY THIS for the young: they make it look easy, not their writing
which is still a bright tangle of forms, a knitted bric-a-brac of imagery.
Sheer raw talent still needs experience's lathe. No, I am talking
about their selves being more fluid, more woke, more tech-savvy than
me. I envy their cutting-edge fashions and job hopping, *c'est la vie*
idealism. No brands, no figureheads, no institutions seem worthy
of their time, as they prefer to worship curiosity. In their world, if you
can tweet it, it can be done. I am jealous of that potential. The flush
of youth, and not the stoop of middle age. Du Fu said, *Kids get off
my lawn*, which is a loose approximation, but I read their chapbooks,
bathe in their optimism, listen to the new chatter about this season's
next great poet, thinking the kids are alright, even if they only read
each other. Their enthusiasm a flagpole staking ground in the world.
The white hairs in my beard reminding me how it once was mine.

TO REBEL? I TRIED. When your father is a policeman and shows you his revolver when you are fourteen, when your father shoots a fox you notice idling alongside a great northern highway, throws the carcass at your feet so it shits on the truck's floor, all for the price of its pelt, you begin to listen to punk music, to paper the walls of your room with its posters: iconography, faux rebellion. Then you start to stay out late and drink, all your angst blown to smithereens for the time the alcohol lasted. Then you talk back to your mother, her voice hitting a high register, that tone, her red face distorted with outrage and furor, as you stomp downstairs to your bedroom. Now what? I'm fifty. My students tell me I sold out. When I try to protest all modern revolutions have reinforced the power of the State, they roll eyes, too busy hating stepparents, plotting the violent overthrow of the patriarchy, imagining puppet strings cut. *Viva la revolución!*

I FEEL A MILD COMPASSION for all things as I get older. The old agonies hurt less. My new love is a luxury not to be taken for granted. I am proud and patient for the first time in my life. A father whose love for his children is egoless and irrepressible. Infinite. So why this change, this better self? Could it be I am happy and content, so late in life that the old worn-out feelings are suddenly nimble and fresh again? Lately, mind and heart speak as one. I love sitting out on our deck with Aura and our dog Truman doing nothing as important as enjoying the chill in the spring air. No burden of understanding, nor craving for reality, more than that. Gone are the bad old days, monstrous and awful. We exist in the world, and love's god-glimmer augments it. So now we sit warming ourselves by this small fire, hands held under a thick blanket, watching our dog nose a back fence, and I think maybe Eros is enough to cure one's ailments, or *all* ailments, our love composed of lofty stuff.

I AM TRYING NOT to lie to you, trying not to say I am a body
that breaks into blossom whenever I see horses, like James
Wright famously wrote. I once believed in the psalmic line,
which is one way to get out of one's self; alcohol is another.
Some poets use both. I certainly did, until neither worked
anymore. Things detached from names can be seen, witnessed,
but naming things sates the hunger God's absence leaves. Poetry
is two parts pilgrimage, one part education. The shrines are
different for everyone—childhood, the past, the Edenic place,
maybe the unthawed snow burying a neighbourhood in 1975.
All of it deserves its share of worship, of praise, despite half
the people sleeping in those houses in 1975 now being extinct.
Even the World War II veteran who sold us pop and chips
out of the back of the Legion. Stan with his one good eye.

DESIRE, LOVE, LONGING and happiness: all are tempered in middle age's forge. We surge forward after these titanic forces with all the fervour of youth, then cry theft when they retreat from us, not realizing until much later, when we are quite older, they underlie most things. Jack Gilbert knew it. He sat on a Greek island until he felt the unusual heft of his contentment overtake his thoughts. Twenty years ago I wanted to write about great things, but now it is enough to feel them waking in me, the light in my yard revealing my own bright hungers. The fence shall be mended. The spirit shall remember its agency. Dandelions poke through fresh grass like yellow bulletins from another world. How am I happy and whole again after years of sadness? *The sadness makes you fine,* I hear Gilbert's poems whisper, and I remember waking years ago on Naxos, the blue and white of the buildings, places hewn from ancient volcanic rock, thinking the Aegean had sewn its moody allure into me.

IT IS TRUE the world is full of sorrows, and podcasts, and that my memories will eventually go down with the ship, all of them, even that time in Rome when I left a friend behind on a subway platform and hopped quickly through a train's sliding doors, his face falling as I hunched my shoulders: all those moments chained to the oars of reminiscence shall go down into the dark without me knowing where any of it was leading. I think death is like a life, unrecollected. The waiting for water to boil, coffee to perk, gas tank to fill, orders to be taken, moments no one remembers but were commonplace and happened. Death has no memory, so why should we? Because the universe remembers every single gravitational wave, because every spring flower blooming remembers winter is over. Memory makes us more visible, more apparent to ourselves, alters us while we are still here, helps us wander this world with its prescriptions, its used appliance stores, its loneliness. Our memories like galaxies birthed and dying in the dark.

WHO ARE WE, together and apart? One nation under money's dusk
and the "I" roaming the halls of our collective spirits. We meet
at the sense gates, which is to say at the point outside ourselves.
I listen to voices, both outer and inner, a real cinephile addicted
to the theatre of what appears real. Even judgements are figments
for big decisions haunt us. Life is just a modern version of some
old Greek tragedy. Food, war, hatred, love. Just with more Nike
sneakers, sleights of hand and oceans full of microplastics. Am I
the monster in the famous novel, or its brilliant inventor? Words
spool out from the darkness containing little traces of ectoplasm
from the spirit realm. Too bad I don't believe in ghosts. I believe
in what's new. Like rhyming *hoax* with *crux*. Language is a Geiger
counter revealing where is safe and where dangerous. I've tried
to live in both places. My empire, these billion stars all on fire.

I'M ALL OUT OF IDIOMS and apps and breadcrumbs to help me wander these deep dark woods. These perishing fairy-tale days without faeries or happy endings. This is our only paradise and it is fallen. Still, we have each other, even if I let the lawn die without watering it, and the house needs a fresh coat of paint. Why settle for the second-rate? Because we can improve ourselves to the point of forgetting grief or love, which is why I let the dishes pile in the sink and the chore list sits undone, my mind revelling in life's want, my eyes meeting your eyes, my desire not one singular thing but many things, dark wings murmuring above a field. Tomorrow I will put the bookcase together, worship the ersatz, strum depression's black guitar strings, fear climate change. How it sits atop its treasure hoard of unrecycled plastic bottles swishing its tail, thinking of the future, a world on fire. But for today, no fears when I'm with you. The witch is dead. The way out is clear.

I HAVE NO EXCUSES for the way I am. Not my gender, nor the benders
I had on lonely inconsolable nights, nor do I blame my boyhood
waiting at the centre of a dark enchanted forest for a woodcutter
carrying an axe to rescue it. I am stubborn in sobriety and love,
and I will sit here listening to the doves sing dawn into being
at my little table, pushing words back and forth until something
takes a little ragged breath onto the page. I am greedy, and only
by waiting do the images and emphases come. Time heals you
or bleeds you. Time is never enough before disappearing entirely.
I am under orders to wrap this up, so ignore time, and your own
heartburn and sexual hang-ups, and contribute a little beauty or
wonder to the world. Surely, the two of us together can tame luck
and put together a happy ending. Me crying in a forest of dark trees.
You with your silver axe, sprinting to the place where my voice calls.

YOU CANNOT BEAT things into blossom although I have tried stubbornly in my way. *So many poems begin where they should end*, Philip Levine wrote, and so many of my poems begin with endings—childhood, Montreal, a marriage, my drinking, regrets—as these few lines end now one more book without a prayer or prophesy, but only hope I have spoken the right words at least part of the time. The poems bound between covers so they might sleep the dream of a man's life until some reader opens these pages and finds ghosts there. So be it. I regret nothing anymore, not old selves that fled in the night and never came back, not the fallen blossoms left shredded in the yard, not the blood and beaten language piecing this together behind my eyes before letting the words rest on a page for a season, or a century. Let it be enough.

About the Author

CHRIS BANKS is a Canadian poet and author of seven collections of poetry, most recently *Deepfake Serenade* by Nightwood Editions in 2021. His first full-length collection, *Bonfires*, was awarded the Jack Chalmers Award for Poetry by the Canadian Authors Association in 2004. *Bonfires* was also a finalist for the Gerald Lampert Memorial Award for best first book of poetry in Canada. His poetry has appeared in *The New Quarterly*, *Arc Magazine*, *The Antigonish Review*, *Event*, *The Malahat Review*, *GRIFFEL*, *American Poetry Journal* and *PRISM International*, among other publications. He lives and writes in Kitchener, Ontario.

Acknowledgements

I would like to thank the editors of the following magazines for accepting some of these poems often with slightly altered versions in their pages:

American Poetry Journal – "Say Dynamite"

The Ampersand Review – "Sublimity"

GRIFFEL – "Interrogation Room A"

Medium Poet Spotlight – "Ode to Disappearing," "Reality"

Ottawa Poetry Newsletter – "Love Song"

Periodicities – [Do you mind if I get personal? The *I* is just a placeholder], [I never read Berryman's *77 Dream Songs* or Lowell's *Notebook*], [This is not an urn of images, nor is it a proper self-depiction.], [My first poetry love affair was Al Purdy, then Gwendolyn MacEwen.]

Catherine Owen's Magazine – [Desire, love, longing and happiness…]

The Walrus – [I am trying not to lie to you…]

Some of these poems were also published in a chapbook, *Shadow Forecast* (Floodlight Editions, 2021).

The poem "Resemblances" owes a debt of gratitude and inspiration to the poem "Remedy" by Bob Hicok.

Many thanks to my wonderful editor Virginia Konchan, and to Lisa Richter, Lara Egger, Paul Vermeersch, Jim Johnstone, Catherine Owen, Samuel Strathman, Bob Hicok, John Gallaher, Chris Hutchinson, Silas White, rob mclennan, Matt Rader, Emma Skagen, Nightwood Editions, Aura Hertzog for love and support, and my entire family.